WILLY'S CUT AND SHINE

Michael Bradford

BROADWAY PLAY PUBLISHING INC
224 E 62nd St, NY, NY 10065
www.broadwayplaypub.com
info@broadwayplaypub.com

WILLY'S CUT AND SHINE
© Copyright 2005 by Michael Bradford

Cover art by Stefano Imbert

First printing: July 2005
This printing: November 2015
I S B N: 978-0-88145-269-3

Book design: Marie Donovan
Word processing: Microsoft Word
Typographic controls: Xerox Ventura Publisher 2.0 P E
Typeface: Palatino
Printed and bound in the U S A

WILLYS CUT AND SHINE was presented at the Lark Theater as a BareBones Presentation, opening on 27 March 2003. The cast and creative contributors were:

LOUIS/SOLDIER . . . . Chad Boseman
CLAUDE . . . . Chad Coleman
BENNET . . . . .Benard Cummings
SYLVESTER . . . . .Arthur French
NATE . . . . Dondre Greenhouse
SHERIFF/CAPTAIN . . . . .Tom Ligon
HAROLD . . . . Greg Mouning
CHI-TOWN . . . . .Kareem Ra
QUINCEY . . . . Keith Randolph Smith

Director . . . . Daniella Topol

CHARACTERS

QUNICEY, *a veteran of W W II and the brother of the murdered Louis. QUNICEYs mind is continually trying to reconcile his life as a black man in Georgia and the empty price he paid in Europe through the war. He is simply tired and wants nothing more than to lie down beside his murdered brother.*

LOLAR, *he is the dead friend of QUNICEY's, lost in the waning days of the war. LOLAR occupies the world in QUNICEY's mind. He is young, optimistic, rash, full of life.*

CAPTAIN, *the white officer in charge of QUNICEYs company during the war. Along with LOLAR, he occupies a hard fought for space in QUNICEY's mind. The structure, and content, of the play allows for this part to be doubled with SHERIFF FRANK.*

BENNET MOORE, *educated at a college in Boston, back home for varies reasons. Meticulous in appearance and speech, doing no more with his education than dispensing barbershop philosophy.*

SYLVESTER ROY, *retired railroad porter, living on his pension, old and no nonsense, has yet to lose a game of dominoes to HAROLD, and cannot fathom it.*

HAROLD MORRIS, *retired factory worker who spends his days in the barbershop with the fellows. He does enjoy their company, but also has a great desire to avoid his wife. A bit nervous when anything in his life shifts to the left or the right.*

CLAUDE BERRY, *like* QUNICEY, *also veteran of W W II, saw action all over Europe, is home and having a hard time reconciling the freedom he experienced in a foreign country against the lack of freedom at home.*

NATE PORTER, *a young simple man who mentally functions enough to take care of his essential needs, one of which is spending time in the barbershop in order to feel accepted, and the other is gambling away his rent on a regular basis.*

CHI-TOWN, *a young gambler with a drug habit from Chicago, though he is originally from Durham, he has been gone for several years. His grandmother raised him and it is her funeral he comes home for. Having run out of drugs and money, he is stranded, in more ways than one.*

SHERIFF FRANK, *a bit younger than* SYLVESTER. *Not the least bit physically imposing. He and* SYLVESTER *have a history that is as old as they are. The* SHERIFF *is a man who is willing to take the law to the limits set by his "constituents" and no further.*

SET REQUIREMENTS

The drama requires one set, which is the barbershop, and an open acting area for the scenes outside of the shop.

Large set pieces:

a small card table for the domino games
two or three barber's chairs
barber's work stand with mirrors and drawers
a mourners bench (church pew) in the space as well
there is one entrance/exit, which is the door to the shop

PUBLISHER'S NOTE

Special thanks to Mac Wellman for bringing this brilliant playwright to our attention.

ACT ONE

(Scene opens, lights full up with the bang of a domino on table. Willy's Barbershop, Durham, Georgia, 1950, unseasonably cold. Two chairs and barber tables with mirrors and all the requisite utensils of a barber, a mourner's bench and a card table. Newspapers are everywhere. The barber, BENNET MOORE, is busy cleaning his clippers. HAROLD MORRIS and SYLVESTER ROY are busy at a game of dominoes.)

SYLVESTER: What that look like? Huh? Look like fifteen to me. Get on the train or get left! Five, ten, fifteen. *(Writes down the score.)*

HAROLD: That hurt, didn't it?

SYLVESTER: Hurt? Hurry up and lay down that funky five-one. I'm doing business here.

BENNET: And where have you been hiding, Claude?

CLAUDE: Had to make a run to Clarkson, damn truck broke down.

HAROLD: Seem like by now you'ld a come to the fact you ought to take better care of your shit and then you wouldn't...

CLAUDE: Seem like everyday now I'm more tired of people in general, but you in particular, Harold.

HAROLD: Why is it the evil, crazy Negroes, is the ones that live forever? Hmm? Now you seen them war reels, Negroes in them boats or what ever the hell they was, 'bout to hit the beach? They either gets shot *'fore* they hit the water, shot *in* the water, or shot *on* the damn beach, matter fact I'm still trying to figure out how we even won the war 'cause it look like everybody got shot! and for damn sho' you'd think dime to dollar, between Quincey and Claude, one of these Negroes would'a got shot in the ass!

(HAROLD *lays down a bone and* SYLVESTER *quickly follows with another.*)

SYLVESTER: Whoa! What is that? That fifteen? Five, ten, fifteen. I'll write it down, I got the pad.

CLAUDE: You know you spent many a sleepless night worryin' 'bout me and Quincey!

SYLVESTER: All of Harold's nights is sleepless, wondering whether or not Helen gone stab his ass.

BENNET: How many years has it been now, Mister Harold, and Helen is still a bit jealous?

SYLVESTER: Please! Don't be for Helen, Harold and the virgin Mary be thick as thieves.

HAROLD: Only reason I'm married right now is cause I was tired, bent down to catch my breath and when I stood up, Helen was standing there with the justice of the peace. Shoot, Helen know. I cain't even go back to the state of Louisiana! I swear they's fifteen geetchie waiting for me at the state line right now.

SYLVESTER: If you ever play a bone well as you lie, you might'a fooled up and won a game in the last twenty years.

BENNET: The monster under the bed is often much larger than the one who is literally at the front door.

(*Every one stops to look at* BENNET *before they all fall out.*)

HAROLD: What in the hell is he talking about?

CLAUDE: Damn Bennet!

BENNET: Mister Sylvester, are you prepared to tighten up that line in the back today?

SYLVESTER: I'm a little busy whipping Harold's ass, right now.

CLAUDE: You better leave him alone, Bennet. You see how his temples was jumping trying to get that last fifteen!

SYLVESTER: Don't rattle your change while I'm counting dollars, youngsta. You can get some of this when I'm through with Harold.

(The phone rings.)

HAROLD: I ain't here.

BENNET: *(Answers the phone)* Willy's Cut and Shine...I'm sorry Helen, no, Helen, he isn't here...soon as he get here, Helen...likewise, Helen. *(Hangs up phone)*

HAROLD: "Soon as he get here?" Did I say anything about "soon as I get here?"

BENNET: I'm a little tired of telling the same lie for you everyday. I thought I might change up.

HAROLD: You don't know how I set that up or backed it up. I might have something going on next week I'm setting ground work for...

CLAUDE: Groundwork?

HAROLD: That's what I said, groundwork. You don't know what I'm talkin' 'bout here.

SYLVESTER: Please! Every Negro in here, 'cept you Harold, know something 'bout *groundwork*!

HAROLD: See, that's why you Negroes always getting caught in some shit you ain't got no business in, 'cause you know too damn much.

CLAUDE: *(Laughing)* Helen know your ass is sitting right here. Where else you gone be?

SYLVESTER: He play like he ain't here!

CLAUDE: One these days she gone show up, then what you gone do?

BENNET: When a woman wants you, you cannot run and you cannot hide.

SYLVESTER: Watch the board, Harold.

HAROLD: Give me five. And whether or not I'm here, ain't the issue.

BENNET: Enlighten us.

HAROLD: The issue is, you cain't be jumping every time no woman call.

CLAUDE: You jump every time the phone ring!

SYLVESTER: Everytime.

HAROLD: Helen know when I step out the house, where I goes is my business.

CLAUDE: Helen catch you in the wrong spot that's yo' ass.

SYLVESTER: You waiting on Jesus to play that five-one, Harold?

HAROLD: Quit looking at my hand, Sylvester.

SYLVESTER: Ain't nobody worried 'bout yo' hand. Hell, I know what you got five minutes after I set up! YOU don't know what you got, don't know what to do with what you got. Which is why I been whipping yo' ass for the past thirty-two years.

BENNET: You are looking a bit rough through the neck, Mister Sylvester. It might be prudent to line it up before...

(NATE PORTER *enters and goes to the window.*)

NATE: Bennet.

BENNET: Nate.

HAROLD: *(Slaps a "bone" down hard)* Give me ten!
Whatn't looking for that was you?

SYLVESTER: Ten? Negro, that bad eye getting worse
every day. That's five.

HAROLD: Just write it down!

SYLVESTER: *(In the midst of writing)* Write it down?
I'm writing it down, with yo' blind ass. Bennet,
how old you think I am?

(Immediately puts up his hand to keep CLAUDE *from
answering.* NATE *moves from the window to the empty
barber's chair.)*

SYLVESTER: I ain't ask you, Claude.

BENNET: I'd say you are kicking sixty-five in the gluteus
maximus, Mister Sylvester.

HAROLD: Whose day was it to bring the dictionary?

*(NATE moves from the chair to the window and back to the
chair.)*

NATE: Ass. That's latin for ass.

HAROLD: Nate, you cain't count change, how the hell
you know latin?

SYLVESTER: Seen two wars....

CLAUDE: Sylvester Roy, you know you was punching
tickets on the midnight dog in '44! I would say you
been as far as Boston, but I put money on the fact yo'
country ass probably never got off the train! Now how
you seen two wars from a train?

SYLVESTER: Don't worry how I seen two wars, I seen two wars, fool-and three wives...

HAROLD: From yo' back yard.

SYLVESTER: I got to go overseas to see something?

CLAUDE: You ain't seen no war. Ain't nothing else like it in the world.

SYLVESTER: You don't know what I'm talking 'bout. You got to put in some time on God's green 'fore you know what I'm talking 'bout. These two hands cut more dead Negroes out of trees that any one of you fools even know. You don't know nothing bout midday snatchings and midnight lynchings. Nothing 'bout mole piss and vinegar and white powder by the front door. Everytime you open your mouth "the war" fall out, but when you seen what I seen, you gets what they calls common mother wit sense. Which comes in handy when I'm trying to figure out whether or not I need my neck lined up! Give me ten.

BENNET: Did you say mole urine and...

(NATE *leaves the bench for the window again.*)

NATE: *(Nervous)* Louis coming through here today?

SYLVESTER: Young Rockefella ain't made his appearance yet.

BENNET: You are aware Mister Louis does not care for that term.

SYLVESTER: I don't like okra but it keep you humble, don't it?

CLAUDE: I don't know how you eat that mess. And what is all that slimy shit dripping off...

HAROLD: Fry it. Only way to eat okra and keep it down. Get you a corn meal batter, fry it deep. You might be able to keep that down. Then again it ain't bad in some oxtail stew, my Aunt Lillian...

SYLVESTER: The light one?

HAROLD: Right, right, she got to have it once't a week, but don't mess 'round have one them geetchies work it in some gumbo for you, course you got to be careful 'bout any kind'a red sauce a geetchie try to give ya', I ever tell you....

SYLVESTER: Harold!

HAROLD: What?

SYLVESTER: You wanna play a bone 'fore you start lying?

HAROLD: (*Slams down a domino*) I don't know what you was in such a hurry fo'. Most folk try to run in the *opposite* direction of a ass whipping. What is that? Five, ten, fifteen. You want me to write that down?

(SYLVESTER *writes down score.*)

HAROLD: Louis come through here everyday, don't he, Nate?

CLAUDE: Rent check a little short again, Nate?

NATE: I seen him going into Wilmont's Hardware yesti'day, right through the front do', look like he was picking up some shoe polish, so I thought he was coming through here.

CLAUDE: That's why yo' ass whatn't here yesti'day.

HAROLD: What in the hell is he going up into Wilmots for? Get what he need from Simpsons like everybody else.

BENNET: When is the last time Simpson had something you needed, when you needed it?

HAROLD: He got plenty, and nine million catalogues to order whatever he *ain't* got...

CLAUDE: Take Simpson a week to order it and two mo'
for it to come in. *(Pause)* A man oughtta' get what he
want when he want it.

SYLVESTER: Ain't got nothing to do with what *is*,
or what *ain't* on the shelves, Louis think cause he
got some money he ain't got to....

CLAUDE: This ain't got *nothing* to do with money!

SYLVESTER: Then what he going in there for? And
you know good and well what I'm talkin' 'bout here,
Claude. Louis ain't got no damn business going into
Wilmot's Hardware! He forget who he is sometimes.

HAROLD: *(Slaps a bone down hard)* Nate, was that you
peeking in the window yesti'day afternoon?

SYLVESTER: *(Slaps a bone down hard)* Nate don't know
what he did five minutes ago, let alone yesti'day.

NATE: *(He moves to the empty barber's chair.)* You don't
know when he coming through today?

BENNET: I am not privy to Mr. Louis' work schedule,
if that is what you're asking.

HAROLD: *(Pointing to the window)* Look like Louis
coming 'cross the street right now.

NATE: *(He rushes back to the window, the sound of a car
can be heard.)* Aww naw, naw, naw!

SYLVESTER: Nate, tell the man the Mill put you off.
Louis ain't never put nobody on the street behind
no money.

NATE: *(Looking out the window, the sound of a car moves
from left to right.)* Who, who own a purple deuce and
a quarter?

CLAUDE: Nobody in here.

HAROLD: Tuck Wilmont.

SYLVESTER: Get out the window, Nate.

NATE: Yep, there go Tuck Wilmont.

(SYLVESTER, HAROLD, BENNET, and CLAUDE all go to the window.)

CLAUDE: What the hell Tuck Wilmot doing on this isde of town?

HAROLD: Is that a...shotgun?

(The sound of two shotgun blasts, pause then another. After a moment, the sound of a car engine gunning and roaring off.)

NATE: ....awww naw naw naw! *(The men stand in frozen silence for a moment.)*

CLAUDE: Help me get him out the street.

(CLAUDE exits with NATE to get LOUIS.)

HAROLD: Good God a'mighty. Did you see that.

SYLVESTER: I'm standing right here, ain't I?

BENNET: *(He moves for the phone.)* I'm calling Meeks.

SYLVESTER: Doctor Meeks? I don't care how much money Louis got, we cain't take him to Meeks' office.

HAROLD: You might as well gone on, call George Clifford.

BENNET: Meeks'll come here.

SYLVESTER: *(Looking out the window at the two men working, does not bother to turn to the conversation.)* Meeks ain't coming here. You know who was in that car? Tuck Wilmot! Meeks ain't coming here. Not for this. What about Randolph?

BENNET: Randolph know what the hell he's doing? He don't know nothing about cutting on nobody!

SYLVESTER: He was a war medic, cut on Negroes's everyday!

BENNET: *(Moves back to the window, pointing to the action on the street)* A Medic? That was a shotgun!

(NATE and CLAUDE make it to the door with LOUIS. BENNET hands him a barber sheet.)

HAROLD: I tol' you, you might as well call George, hell I seen it from the window .....

CLAUDE: I swear to God, Harold!

SYLVESTER: Shotgun. Laid his chest wide open.

(NATE slowly moves from the body to stand alone downstage, looking at his hands.)

HAROLD: That's a lot of blood, Syl. I ain't never seen that much blood.

NATE: I would'a paid him, I whatn't back but a month, I would'a....this is bad, this is bad.

SYLVESTER: Shut up, Nate.

(BENNET picks up the phone.)

BENNET: I'm calling his wife.

SYLVESTER: Is you crazy? Everybody standing here know who was in that car.

CLAUDE: There's a murdered man on the floor! We just gone stand here?

BENNET: *(Clicks for a dial tone then dials)* All right! This is it. I'll call George Clifford at the funeral home. Tell him to come get Louis. When he get here, we tell him to mind his business. Clifford's good at that. Somebody needs to go over to Mountain Street, tell Mrs Louis what we got here and...George, yeah, listen...

HAROLD: Goin' in and out of Wilmot's, you cain't just go in and out there like that, you cain't....

CLAUDE: Harold, I need one mo' word from you. One mo'.

SYLVESTER: You just cain't tell no woman...

CLAUDE: That's the man's wife, Sylvester Roy.

SYLVESTER: You ain't got no idea what that woman will do! She liable to run all the way over to Wilmot's Hardware and....

BENNET: *(Hangs up the phone)* George ought to be here in a minute.

SYLVESTER: She don't need to know nothing about the car.

CLAUDE: She got a right to know....

BENNET: When we got to the window the car was gone.

CLAUDE: She don't need to know nothing 'bout all of us standing in the window watching Louis' murder! Huh? Nothing 'bout Tuck Wilmot and that purple deuce and a quarter?! That what you mean to say?

BENNET: I said what I mean.

CLAUDE: We can go over to there right now. Wilmots. Right now.

SYLVESTER: You and nobody else going nowhere 'cause you know big timber from brush, don't you? Now we gone take care of this like we always do. George Clifford gone do what he do, we gone put Louis in the ground, better than the average jack-leg negroe we ever cut out a tree. We gone cry and shout and then we gone go home to a house that's still standing in a neighborhood that ain't burning. That's what I'm gone do and that's what Claude's gone do.

CLAUDE: You better call Franks, then.

SYLVESTER: What for?

CLAUDE: *(Pointing to* LOUIS*)* You need another reason? What you think Quincey gone do? Hmmm? That's the man's brother. You don't wanna tell the man's wife, what in the hell you gone tell Quincey?

HAROLD: And he was crazy *'fore* he left for the war.

SYLVESTER: I'm gone call Sheriff Frank and tell him what? Tuck Wilmot just opened up a hole in Louis bigger'n the state of Georgia! And what you think Frank gone do?

CLAUDE: What he supposed to do.

SYLVESTER: Don't nothing in the world work like it supposed to! The sooner you figure that out the better you'll feel.

CLAUDE: I just thought 'cause you two was so tight, come up together and all....

SYLVESTER: How the hell a Colored man and a White man come up together in Georgia?

CLAUDE: He better do something, Mister Sylvester. He better do something right quick 'cause I ain't come home to live this no mo'! I don't care how many folk you done cut down outta' trees, I ain't doing this! You better call him. You think Quincey gone sit down for this? Not after what we been through.

SYLVESTER: You ain't been through nothing! You live to be seventy something in Durham County, Georgia, then you talk to me.

HAROLD: (*At the window.*) George Clifford should'a been here. Who going out there, tell Quincey?

(*Everybody looks at* NATE.)

NATE: What?

BENNET: Nate, you need to go out and tell Quincey.

NATE: Why me?

HAROLD: 'Cause yo ass was in the war with him.

NATE: So was fifty thousand other Negroes, so was Claude.

HAROLD: We sho' as hell ain't sending Claude.

NATE: I seen Quincey when he left and when he come home just like the rest of yaw. I ain't set foot outside Fort Hood my entire tour.

SYLVESTER: Thank God, we'd be speaking German right now if yo' silly ass ever found Europe.

NATE: You always got to something to say, don't you Mister Sylvester? Why don't you take your old ass out there. Tell Quincey his brother is laid out full of buckshot, bled out on the floor. Then tell him who did it. Now if he go crazy and kill yo' ass we ain't lost much since you the closet one to the grave anyhow.

SYLVESTER: You gone be a little closer than Louis here you keep....

CLAUDE: You cain't get no closer than this! We just talking here or we doing something?

(Phone rings and BENNET *answers it.)*

HAROLD: I ain't here.

BENNET: Yeah George...naw...you should have been here by now...I don't know George, listen, you know the money will be straight...if it ain't the money, what is it? I don't care what you heard, just come do this...George! *(He hangs up the phone.)*

SYLVESTER: Well what is it?

BENNET: He said he's not coming.

HAROLD: Ain't coming? How the hell George get to be an undertaker

BENNET: Said he heard the shotgun from his shop, didn't know what it was till we called, said he's not coming out the house. We got to bring him.

NATE: *(Staring at the body)* I ain't goin out there. I ain't going. I ain't going nowhere.

SYLVESTER: We ain't asking.

BENNET: You are probably the only one here Quincey can take.

SYLVESTER: Harold, bring your car 'round the front.

HAROLD: You know what kind of mess...you know Helen is liable to...

SYLVESTER: When the last time Helen been in that car? Back seat 'bout to fall through the floorboard! Just bring that raggedy car 'round the front so we can take care of this.

HAROLD: I got plenty family in Baltimore. I need to go home right now and pack! My *sister* live in Baltimore. I swear I'm moving, I swear I'm moving!

(HAROLD *exits and* NATE *starts to follow.*)

SYLVESTER: Where you goin'?

NATE: I'm just gone stand over here by, a...I'm just gone wait by the door, for Harold.

SYLVESTER: That's right. Soon as Harold pull up you and Claude get Louis in the back.

CLAUDE: So that's it? We gone come in here tomorrow play bones cut heads shine shoes like today was any other day?

BENNET: Somebody needs to go by Mountain Street, tell Mrs Louis.

HAROLD: *(He enters.)* Come on the street is clear.

CLAUDE: *(Putting on his coat)* You better call Franks, Sylvester, or to hell with you and everybody else in here.

SYLVESTER: You so fired to put yo' foot in something, Claude? You leave George Clifford's you go by Mountain Street. Tell Mrs Louis where her husband is and then you go home, you hear me! You take your ass straight home. And Nate....

NATE: I got it!

(CLAUDE *and* NATE *exit with the body. The phone rings a few times before* BENNET *snatches it up.*)

BENNET: George? I'm sorry, Helen, this is not a good time. *(He hangs up the phone.)*

HAROLD: *(He steps into the shop.)* What you mean "this ain't a good time?" Do you know Helen liable to get dressed and come down here?

BENNET: Just how would you define the situation, Mister Harold?

HAROLD: Damn! *(Beat. He exits.)*

SYLVESTER: *(Puts on his coat and hat. Staring at the blood spot left by the body.)* Damn Louis...I don't know why in the hell he had to start going up into Wilmots after all this time! He think 'cause he half a Wilmot the ol' man just gone up and say....

BENNET: Louis was a Wilmot?

SYLVESTER: Ain't that what I said. Half anyway. His mama worked for old man Wilmot when Quincey was a boy. She quit right before Louis got here. *(Beat)* Anybody been here long enough, know how this work. You take your ass into Wilmot's Hardware one too many times and they liable to run through this whole side of town like they did them folk in Oklahoma. How you run the kind of business he did and not know that?

BENNET: Maybe he wasn't thinking about...

SYLVESTER: Well he should'a been! How you think we still here after all the hell we been through? This is a

community. We all done swallowed crow for
somebody else. You don't get but so big. *(Beat)* Bennet.

BENNET: Mister Sylvester.

SYLVESTER: *(Stops at the blood)* You better get something
on this blood 'fore it leave a stain. Little lye get that
right up.

BENNET: *(Laughs)* A little lye. Right.

(SYLVESTER *exits.* BENNET *gets a box of powder and
sprinkles it on the floor. Puts away the box, puts on his coat
and hat and exits, stepping a wide swatch around the blood.
Cross fade to an open acting space with* QUINCEY *sitting on
a stool, dressed for the weather, shing a pair of army boots.*
NATE *enters, fingering his hat.)*

NATE: Quincey.

QUINCEY: *(Holds up the boots)* 'fore the war I could fit
these. Went on like butter. Now, I cain't get passed the
toe. I would cut'em right here, but naw...maybe Louis
could wear'em just like...naw.

NATE: What you be doing out here in the midle of
nowhere, Quincey. Took me hour and a half with
Harold's raggedy car, every bump you it feel like
the floorboard gone fall right...

QUINCEY: What you want, Nate?

NATE: How many houses Louis got? Don't make
much sense you out here when....

QUINCEY: I'm sitting here, Nate.

NATE: Right. *(Silence)* Been some trouble.

QUINCEY: Well now you come to exactly what I'm
doing out here, Nate. Ain't my trouble, ain't my
business. If Louis got trouble, he know where I am.
And he know....

NATE: That's what this is, Quincey. Trouble with Louis.

QUINCEY: *(Stops shining.)* Louis ain't been no trouble since the day he come in the world, broke water and ain't come for three days, you hear me? Dry birth! Mama damn near died. Now, that's the last time Louis and trouble been in the same room.

NATE: This ain't the kind of trouble just come out the blue. This the kind of trouble come to you.

QUINCEY: You ain't come out here to tell me nothing 'bout Louis. You hear me? Nothing.

NATE: Louis was coming 'cross the street in front of Willy's, we all seen him and...

QUINCEY: What you come out here for, Nate?

NATE: I'm trying to tell you this Quincey, let me tell you this. *(Beat)* Tuck Wilmot....

QUINCEY: Tuck Wilmot?

NATE: Tuck, he come out of nowhere....

QUINCEY: Naw naw naw I knew Tuck when he was this big...

NATE: I swear it look like he come right out the sun....

QUINCEY: ...I whatn't but seven, used to put both his feet fit in my one hand, naw...

NATE: ...laid him down with a shotgun. Three times, all of'em up in here.

QUINCEY: Couldn't been Louis. I'd a felt that, you hear me? I'd a felt something like that and my Louis always been...clean, he's clean! My Louis 'bout yea tall and got a mole on his left cheek, he got a...

NATE: I'm talking 'bout Louis here! We all seen it, Quincey, I'm sorry but...

QUINCEY: You sorry? You standing there watching my brother get shot down in the street and you sorry?

NATE: He was dead 'fore we even got to the door. We tried to....

QUINCEY: (*Coming off the stool and pushing the boots in* NATE'*s face.*) Who I'm gone give these boots to, huh?

NATE: Now see that's why they sent me, I told Sylvester....

QUINCEY: I brought these back for Louis they just whatn't ready yet. Where is he?

NATE: We took him to George Clifford's.

QUINCEY: When.

NATE: This morning. Probably gone be at George's till the weather break though. Too cold. Grounds too hard. Already broke three picks trying to turn it for Eula Watkins. I got Harold's car. I could take you.

QUINCEY: You go head on.

NATE: You quite a ways from town, Quincey. You liable to freeze to death trying to....

QUINCEY: I told you to go head on, Nate. I feel like walking.

NATE: Alright. I'm gone go head on. You want me to tell George Clifford.... Right. I can come on back whenever you feel....Right.

(NATE *exits. Lighting shift, the soldier is purely from the mind of* QUINCEY. LOLAR *enters with W W II garb, pack, helmet, feet wrapped with cloth so they look like blunt objects, rifle, wobbling walk.*)

LOLAR: (*Grunting in pain and disgust. Yelling. Laughing. Sheds pack, opens portable stool and sits. Shouting across and off stage.*) Quincey!

QUINCEY: What you doing here?

LOLAR: Where else I'm supposed to be?

QUINCEY: You was in that field like a puzzle.

LOLAR: ...in the middle of a field.

QUINCEY: ...piece here, piece there...

LOLAR: Right where you left me.

QUINCEY: I tol' you...keep your ass in the ditch with me.

LOLAR: *(Trying to get his boots off)* Arggh! Look at these boots.

QUINCEY: I got my own to worry 'bout. I ain't got time for you right now.

LOLAR: You ain't got time? You think 'cause you left me to go rotten in that field, that was the end of it?

QUINCEY: Why you keep fucking with me? We did all we was supposed to do and more than that! You running 'cross that field...for what?

LOLAR: It all comes around, I swear if it ain't but one true thing in the universe, that's it, it all comes around. And you come back to it the way you left it.

QUINCEY: You skipping yo' piece back puzzle ass cross the universe and you come back with this? I need a word, Lolar! You stepping with angels and saints, listening to choirs sing out shit so sweet we cain't even hear it! And this is all you bring me? I need a word!

LOLAR: Where you put the peaches?

QUINCEY: What peaches?

LOLAR: I know yo' little narrow ass had some peaches, I seen the box.

QUINCEY: This ain't the weather for peaches.

LOLAR: *(Continually at the wrapping on his shoes, grunting)* Like I'm gone chase yo' ass with these feet.

QUINCEY: I look like I'm running?

LOLAR: They say charity start at home.

QUINCEY: Tol' you to stay in the ditch!

LOLAR: What for? You Southern Negroes ain't worth shit. Every nappy headed trick step off a bus at basic. Ain't hit the bricks but a day and that's all you hear! "I cain't wait to git' back home." "Oh, they treats you like family down home." "Oh, my peoples ain't nothing but hospitable back home."

QUINCEY: I'm tired, you hear me?

LOLAR: (Gingerly, starting to unravel the wrapping around his boots. Continually grunting, out of breath, every movement a chore.) One damn peach! You been hiding 'cause yo' brother sent you that box of peaches!

QUINCEY: I ain't got no peaches, I ain't never had... This ain't the weather!

LOLAR: You right. This ain't the weather. You know the last peach I had? Cooper's K-rats peach cobbler. You 'member Cooper?

QUINCEY: Cooper got hit in the water.

LOLAR: That whole first day, last thing on my mind was eating, and then Cooper washed up and just like that, I was starving.

QUINCEY: All that time in the water, his boots was ruint when I seen him.

LOLAR: You know why it took him a day to wash up? K-rats! That Negro was loaded down with k-rats, but, but the peach cobbler is all I took. He had meat loaf and peas and fruit cocktail...You still got that picture?

QUINCEY: No.

LOLAR: The hell you don't!

(Laughing loud and heavy. QUINCEY, head down, pulls a picture out of his shirt pocket.)

LOLAR: Yeah. That's it. I knew you had it.

QUINCEY: You seen it.

LOLAR: You owe me!

QUINCEY: I don't owe you nothing.

LOLAR: C'mon Q, let me see it.

(QUINCEY *puts the picture down in the shadow area. Soldier picks it up quickly, stares at it, rubs his crotch.*)

LOLAR: Damn! Say her name, you know, how you say it.

QUINCEY: It's on the back.

LOLAR: You 'member the last little village we went through in France? How the women ran out and licked us like we was chocolate and we ain't mind a bit!

QUINCEY: I seen her from the street.

LOLAR: *(Straining with his finger over the letters on the back of the picture.)* De...De...

QUINCEY: She had a little flat over that burnt out grocer.

LOLAR: De...De...shit! C'mon, Q! De'la...

QUINCEY: She had skin like, like the color of milk just before you make the cream rise and....

LOLAR: *(Staring at the picture)* Deliqua! Yeah, that's it. What she let you do?

QUINCEY: None of your business.

LOLAR: *(Grinning hard)* The basket thing, you know, on the swing and...

QUINCEY: I said none of your....

LOLAR: Why ain't you call us? Me and Cooper, you should have called us.

QUINCEY: You don't know what all I had to put down just to walk up in there! Every piece of burden put on

me, all the burden I picked up for no damn reason,
just to put my hands on that skin, skin that was just
skin, skin waiting for me to lay down wit' it, waiting
to smother me up in all the sweet shit that ever rose
up in the world, and I'm thinking 'bout calling you?

LOLAR: *(Moaning, on the verge of orgasm)* Damn, she had
big calves, I like me some big calves. A lot of brothers
won't say they be getting with big women, but you give
me a big woman and...

QUINCEY: Put it down.

LOLAR: You don't want it.

QUINCEY: *(Notices the soldier rubbing his crotch again.)*
Put it down.

LOLAR: Calves thick as peaches ain't they?

QUINCEY: I said put it down!

LOLAR: Fuck a peach. I don't even like peaches! *(Pause)*
I got something better than a picture, better than a
peach. *(Instead of the picture, soldier slams down a .45.)*

QUINCEY: *(He backs up.)* I don't owe you nothing!
No peaches no nothing.

LOLAR: Piece of thunder like this, break the weather!

QUINCEY: Yo ass is puzzle pieces going rotten in a field!
I wished to hell it meant something but it don't. Cooper
washing up like driftwood, my brother dead in the
street and it don't mean nothing, NOTHING!

LOLAR: That ain't the truth, you know that ain't the
truth, skin like milk when the cream is rising and...

QUINCEY: I cain't do shit about the weather! That's the
truth. I got to go.

LOLAR: Go! Ain't nobody holding you. But every
morning you wake up you done let a piece of what
we made slip away and cain't nobody say we whatn't

there! can't nobody say we ain't whomp the Third
Reich's ass! But that's what they want to do, ain't it?
They wanna say we whatn't there 'cause low-rate
Negroes like you wanna lay down when it's time to
get up. It's time to get up!

QUINCEY: I stood up! You tell me what it mean! Huh?
I need a word, Lolar! I mean, you come up out the ditch
and run like hell 'cross a field or crossed a street 'till
your legs say to hell with you and all you get is cut to
puzzle pieces or a shotgun is busy making a country
in your chest! I stood up! Sent a lot German boys to
they grave and I'm mo' tired now than I ever was!
I put Louis in the ground then I'm through! I'm gone
lay myself out and let God to skip my ass across the
universe like one them perfect little skipping rocks,
three, fo' times....then oblivion.

LOLAR: *(Mocking* QUINCEY*)* "Louis, I'm gone make it
home for Louis...."

QUINCEY: Fuck you, Louis ain't never need what I got
to give! Louis is....

LOLAR: *(Holds up .45. He rises wobbly, full of pain, starts to
exit.)* Waiting for the weather to break! I might be lying
'bout everything, 'bout you and me and Cooper and
the peaches and the boots. But not this, Q. I swear,
you cain't plant nothing good in this weather. Nothing.
You gone need this.

*(*LOLAR *leaves the .45 and exits.* QUINCEY *grabs his coat,
packs the boots and cleaning gear in small bag. He stands
staring at the .45. Maybe* Come On into My Kitchen
or some other blues begins to play in the cross fade from
QUINCEY *to the "*Willy's." *Lights fade back up half as*
BENNET *enters, hangs his coat, pulls out a broom and dust
pan, sweeps the powder over the blood spot to no avail. Puts
the gear back, begins to set up his barber gear, lights slowly
rise to full.* SYLVESTER *and* HAROLD *enter, take a wide step*

over the blood, hang up their coats. SYLVESTER *sits at their table to set up the bones,* HAROLD *moves too the window.)*

BENNET: Sylvester, Harold.

SYLVESTER/HAROLD: Bennet.

SYLVESTER: You put some lye on that?

BENNET: Indeed.

(NATE *enters and is mesmerized by the blood.)*

BENNET: Mister Nate.

NATE: Bennet. *(Beat)* You stand here long enough, seem like you can still kind'a see Louis.

BENNET: Come on here and sit down, Nate.

(NATE *sits in the empty barber's chair.* HAROLD *rises and moves to the window.)*

SYLVESTER: You talk to Quincey?

NATE: Yesterday.

HAROLD: Well what did the man say, Nate?

NATE: Said he felt like walking.

HAROLD: Walking! You ain't the man back to town? That's damn near twenty miles!

SYLVESTER: You in a hurry to see Quincey?

HAROLD: What about Claude? You seen Claude?

NATE: Whatn't looking for'em.

HAROLD: I ain't ask you if you was looking for'em, I say did you see him? Damn, Nate.

NATE: I ain't seen'em!

HAROLD: Did you go by Wilmot's?

NATE: I ain't got no reason to be way over there. I come down Mercy, 'cross 5th, then...

HAROLD: Been two days. Ain't nobody seen Claude
since we left Georges. And Quincey...Claude do
something, you don't think he'd come back here,
do you?

SYLVESTER: Well it...

HAROLD: I mean you don't think he's that big a fool?

SYLVESTER: Seem like.....

HAROLD: I see that Negro running up in here I swear
I'm going home and pack my bags! *(Pause)* You think
he would?

SYLVESTER: Yes, Harold, Claude do something, he's
coming straight here! Now get out the window!

HAROLD: I ain't playing Syl, I swear....

(The phone rings.)

HAROLD: I ain't been here.

BENNET: Willy's Cut and Shine...I'm sorry Helen...
you just missed him...I don't know...yes...yes...
goodbye Helen.

HAROLD: Bennet, did I just say....

BENNET: I can't keep up where you have been, where
you haven't been, where you are going to be.

(HAROLD returns to the window.)

SYLVESTER: You see him?

HAROLD: See who?

SYLVESTER: Who you think I'm talkin' 'bout?

HAROLD: Well we working up some options, ain't we?
You could be talking 'bout Quincey 'cause he was crazy
'fore he went overseas and ain't got the little bit of sense
he left here wit' and we ain't got no idea if he coming or
he ain't or he froze dead on the side of the road, or then

there's Claude's crazy ass, and there's the good Sheriff
Frank who's useless as tits on a bull, 'course you say
you ain't too worried 'bout Tuck Wilmot but he liable
to still have a bad taste in his mouth, and then there's
the everyday lynch mob, not to mention I barely made
it out the house today—Helen could be coming down
the street! So who you asking me about?

SYLVESTER: Claude. Do you see Claude?

HAROLD: I'm moving to Baltimore. We need to hurry
up and get Louis in the ground 'fore somebody do
something they ain't got no business....anybody heard
when funeral is?

NATE: Funeral's cancelled.

HAROLD: Nate it's a mistake to send your ass to the
river for water!

NATE: I ain't lying! I seen George Clifford at Simpson's
Store and that's what he said.

SYLVESTER: You know they cain't bury nobody in this
weather?

HAROLD: *(Returns to the window)* How long you think it
take Quincey to get here?

SYLVESTER: Ain't but one reason Quincey ever come in
here and that reason's laid out at George Clifford's.

HAROLD: Quincey liable to have a flashback and kill
everybody in sight, 'cluding me and you!

SYLVESTER: You the one he say he don't like.

HAROLD: Damn, Sylvester!

SYLVESTER: Harold, you 'bout to 'cause me a nervous
breakdown! I been knowing Quincey since he come
in the world. His mama and Louis only thing kept
him here this long, and his mama been gone for a while

now. We put Louis in the ground, we liable to never hear from Quincey again.

(Door opens and scares HAROLD *nearly to death.* CHI-TOWN *steps in, young, a gambler, clean, hair laid to the side, continually sniffing and checking his nose with his handkerchief.)*

CHI-TOWN: What the hell? Look like somebody lost a little something here. *(Steps over the blood as if it is a deep trench, looking back at it, down it.)* Somebody gone clean this up?

BENNET: Won't come up.

CHI-TOWN: Little soap and water...

BENNET: Did that.

CHI-TOWN: You ought'a mix some lye with some yella' root and...

BENNET: Tried that.

CHI-TOWN: My granma had this...

BENNET: I said it won't come up.

CHI-TOWN: *(To* SYLVESTER *and* HAROLD*)* He get excited easy, don't he?

SYLVESTER: *(To* HAROLD*)* Do you know this fool?

*(*NATE *is slowly raising the paper above his face.)*

BENNET: A person with anything resembling intelligence might find it prudent to check his conversation in the company of strangers.

CHI-TOWN: *(To everyone else but* BENNET, *grinning)* Who the hell he supposed to be?

BENNET: I would be the one who unlocks the door to this establishment in the morning and locks it in the evening. I would be the one who accepts the monetary recompense for services rendered. And I would be the one who sets the standard for the oral exchange within these four walls.

CHI-TOWN: Oh, you one them cats keeping warm at night with a book!

SYLVESTER: Harold, would you get out the window.

CHI-TOWN: *(Motions to* HAROLD's *chair.)* Mind if I take a squat? Look like your partner's a bit occupied.

HAROLD: You sit in my chair you gone be occupied.

CHI-TOWN: *(Slowly pushes the chair back in.)* All right then.

SYLVESTER: Harold, get out the damn window and sit down!

CHI-TOWN: *(Motions to the barber chair.)* Can I get a cut, or ahh, is this somebody's chair too?

*(*BENNET *motions for him to sit, drapes barber sheet over him.)*

HAROLD: *(Returns to his chair)* Shit! Here come Claude now.

CLAUDE: *(He enters, wide step over the blood, and spends a moment looking out the window before he sits.)* Bennet.

BENNET: Claude.

HAROLD: *(Tight laugh)* Where you been hiding, Claude?

CLAUDE: You paying my rent, Harold?

SYLVESTER: Where's Tuck Wilmont?

NATE: I don't know why you all are so scared of death.

HAROLD: Ain't nobody scared of death.

SYLVESTER: Where's Tuck Wilmot?

NATE: Ain't like you gone get out of dying.

CLAUDE: I hear they finally broke ground....

NATE: Naw, cracked another pick this morning.

SYLVESTER: I said where is....

NATE: See that's what I'm trying to say, you know you gone be over to George's one day, you might as well go on and live like a....

SYLVESTER: Nate please! Claude, you hear me talking to you!

CLAUDE: Where you think he is? Standing where he always standing this time of the day, behind the counter at Wilmot's Hardware. Bennet standing behind the same barber chair, you and Harold playing the same damn game and Louis is....

SYLVESTER: Is dead! It's done and I don't wanna hear nothing else about it! Louis waiting on the ground to open up. That's it! We put him in it then it's done.

NATE: Ain't natural. That' why the ground won't open up, that's why the blood won't come up, that's why....

SYLVESTER: Neither one of you fools know the first thing 'bout what that was out there! That business was between them two men, Louis and Wilmot. Period!

CHI-TOWN: (*Pause. Makes the production out of the silk handkerchief to wipe his nose.*) Whew! Hawk is flying for sho', ain't it? Seem like don't nothing go like it supposed to down here! I ain't never know Georgia to get cold like this.

HAROLD: (*He slams a bone down, speaks to* CHI-TOWN) I suppose they don't get weather like this where you come from?

CHI-TOWN: (*Pats his pockets.*) Chicago! Don't matter what the weather be like, it's always right.

SYLVESTER: Chicago? Six trains a day run a mainline straight to Chicago. 'less both your pocket's a bit thin...

CHI-TOWN: I'm doing all right. Ain't that right, Home-Boy?

(HAROLD: *Slaps* NATE'S *paper.* CLAUDE *gets up from the mourner's bench, snatching* NATE'S *paper.*)

HAROLD: You know yo' ass cain't read.

NATE: *(Nervous)* Give me the sports section.

HAROLD: Nate, you ain't lost all yo' money, have you?

NATE: I ain't lost no money!

CHI-TOWN: *(Laughing)* Sho'you'right! He know exactly where his money is!

HAROLD: Nate, how you got money to gamble but you ain't got money for rent?

CHI-TOWN: Tell the brother I tried to leave you a little pocket change. Shot a whole game with my left hand, but he insisted I take that too.

SYLVESTER: That's why his simple ass...

NATE: *(Pushes paper down into lap.)* I ain't simple!

SYLVESTER: Well Nate, seem kind of obvious you simply can't shoot no pool. You simply broke, and if it don't be for the fact Miss Louis don't even know what property Louis had to collect rent on, yo' ass would simply be on the street!

CLAUDE: You better watch out, Sylvester Roy. Nate gone jump yo' old ass one day.

SYLVESTER: I wish he would. Ain't got to worry about getting up the rent in a coffin.

CHI-TOWN: Somebody gone have to start paying rent, the way they piling up at Mister Clifford's.

(Silence for a moment)

HAROLD: *(Phone rings.)* I ain't here.

BENNET: Willy's Cut and Shi-... Yes Helen... No, no
Helen... Indeed, soon as he gets here. Goodbye Helen.

SYLVESTER: *(Slaps a bone down)* Give me ten.

BENNET: Why don't you at least give the man back his
rent money? One might make the argument that Mister
Nate is hardly capable of making the wisest decisions.

CHI-TOWN: Look grown, act grown, must be grown.

NATE: Joe Louis getting ready for another fight.

SYLVESTER: That Negroe's broke as Nate.

CLAUDE: You know how much money Joe *gave* the
gov'ment through the war? How the hell Joe Louis
gone be broke?

CHI-TOWN: Cause he's stupid. Don't know when to
leave the game.

HAROLD: You get hit in the head that many times,
you be stupid too.

BENNET: Why does the man have to be stupid? The man
has probably lost more money than you have ever
made, but he's stupid.

SYLVESTER: *(Laughing)* You hear'em after his last fight?
"What happened in there, Joe?" "Uh." "Fifth round was
rough whatn't it, Joe?" "Uh." "Is you broke, Joe?" "Uh."
Ezzard wore his ass out!

NATE: Joe got money's mammy stashed somewhere up
in Harlem.

HAROLD: He get hit in the head again, somebody gonna
have to help him find it!

BENNET: Because he's living simple, like everyday
people, he has to be stupid.

CHI-TOWN: Hell yeah! Who the hell wanna live like
"everyday folk?" Get yours and catch the first train

smoking out of—coonsville. Look here, three, four big money fights tops and I'm through.

CLAUDE: (*Sarcastic.*) A good conk, a pair of Stacey Adams set you 'bout right, huh?

CHI-TOWN: Naw, I'm a come on down here, find me a porch and eat watermelon all day long with you.

(*Silence for a moment,* CLAUDE *glaring and* CHI-TOWN *smiling.*)

BENNET: Pray tell, who is the mighty Joe Louis fighting next?

NATE: Mar-cee-an-oh.

HAROLD: I like Joe but he better keep his ass up in Harlem. That Marciano boy hits like a freight train.

SYLVESTER: Harold, you are the slowest Negro I ever met. You gone play that bone or not?

CHI-TOWN: You ought'a gone on and let me get the next game. I done all ready run through every Negro at Simpson's. He say this ought to be my next stop. 'Sides, look like it liable to be a Spring for this Negro lay down a bone.

SYLVESTER: Do the trains run in the Spring, Harold?

HAROLD: Winter, Spring, Summer, Fall.

SYLVESTER: Any running North?

HAROLD: Every one.

SYLVESTER: Chicago?

HAROLD: (*Mock surprise. Laughter all around*) Chicago? You wouldn't be talking 'bout...

SYLVESTER: Naw, Harold. I'm just talking 'bout train schedules.

(*Laughter*)

CHI-TOWN: It was me, I'd be talking 'bout how you gone get that blood up. 'Nother round like the last one you gone have to re-plank the floor.

CLAUDE: Wouldn't be worried 'bout that blood. Be thankful it ain't yours.

CHI-TOWN: Worried? You sound like somebody's grandma.

CLAUDE: Could be. Could be your grandma. But I ain't Nate.

CHI-TOWN: Crippled blind crazy eight to eighty! I take yo' money, home-boy. Ain't nothing personal.

HAROLD: Whatn't but two months ago some schoolchildren took Nate's money.

CHI-TOWN: Ain't you waiting on a phone call?

(Silence)

BENNET: Well, Mr. Harold! Sounds as if this young man has never had the paradoxical privilege of being in love.

HAROLD: Ain't been nowhere, ain't seen nothing.

CHI-TOWN: A day on the South side of Chicago is like a day anywhere in the world.

HAROLD: *(Slams a bone down)* Chicago my ass. I know that forehead. You been gone, what, four, five years?

CHI-TOWN: Seven.

HAROLD: *(Throws a thumb in his direction)* You can always mark a Watson by they forehead. That's Eula Watson's grandboy.

BENNET: Eula Watson? I am indeed sorry to hear about your grandmother. You came home for the funeral?

CHI-TOWN: This ain't exactly a vacation spot.

HAROLD: *(Laughing)* This is the very kind of fool you find stumbling down alleys at two in the morning, talking 'bout, "I don't know what happened!"

(All laughing now, CHI-TOWN *smiling.)*

CHI-TOWN: You must be crazy! God ain't made the woman to run me.

SYLVESTER: You probably been ran three, four times and don't even know it.

CHI-TOWN: *(Pointing to* NATE*)* I don't get ran. You must be talking 'bout your boy here!

NATE: You ain't talking 'bout me, just last week I had to tell Agnes Watkins to get out my house!

HAROLD: Nate quit lying!

NATE: I ain't lying, I said, Agnes, you know you better go on, I got to get my rest! Agnes always wanna hang on somebody and I tol' her she cramping my roll, I cain't have....

SYLVESTER: Nate, you ain't got a roll to cramp.

CHI-TOWN: Look here, when I puts it down, sister cain't even wake up 'fore noon. She liable to stumble 'round the house for half a day 'fore she come to and need another hit, "Chi-Town," where you at baby, "Chi-Town!"

HAROLD: Women from here to the coast tell you I know how to handle my business.

CHI-TOWN: *(Looking at the phone.)* Ring! Ring!

CLAUDE: *(Sniffs air, exaggerated. Laughter around the room)* Anybody smell milk? I smell milk. Where you get this Negro from?

HAROLD: You ain't heard the man? Chicago!

CLAUDE: Yo' mama coming home? I mean, for the funeral?

CHI-TOWN: Your guess good as mine.

CLAUDE: *(Grinning)* I ain't seen yo' mama since...

CHI-TOWN: Then you seen her more'n me.

CLAUDE: Hell, we all seen her more'n you.

CHI-TOWN: Come again?

(CLAUDE continues to peruse the paper while CHI-TOWN stares at him.)

CLAUDE: Chi-Town! Your mama still sporting that big, ass?

CHI-TOWN: Is this Negro talking to me?

CLAUDE: It was pretty, whatn't it, Nate?

NATE: *(Leans into the memory, smiling)* Sho'nuff was a...

BENNET: *(Leans back into his chair)* Nate.

NATE: I don't recall.

CLAUDE: *(Talking to the paper)* Seem like the more that ass got tapped, the bigger it got.

CHI-TOWN: *(Smiling)* Oh! You must think you know me 'cause I used to live here.

CLAUDE: 'Fore she left, you see that ass coming a mile away and say, yep, that's Shirley's ass.

BENNET: Claude...

CHI-TOWN: But see, I done seen a bit of the world since I left here....

CLAUDE: *(To the rest of the shop)* Right 'fore we shipped out she come down to Fort Hood.

CHI-TOWN: ...and I learned a thing or two 'bout you "down home *country* Negroes."

CLAUDE: How long was that line, Nate?

NATE: I whatn't there.

CHI-TOWN: See, 'till you actually call the shot...

CLAUDE: About a mile, whatn't it?

CHI-TOWN: ...or lay down that bluff, funky hand...

CLAUDE: Even from the back of the line, I said to myself, yep, that's Shirley's ass.

BENNET: Claude!

CHI-TOWN: ...it don't mean shit! *(Calmly)* You probably mad 'cause by the time you got up to the spot, she closed up shop. But if you looking for a line... *(Pats his knife pocket)* ...I got a line for you to stand in, and I try to never disappoint a customer.

CLAUDE: You got a line for me? Look here, one day, me and Johnson and Vashtey was bivwacking on a hill south of Charbonne, France. We was laughing 'cause Johnson thought he saw a German, pissed his pants and emptied his carbine in a deer. Every piece of meat we cut out that deer had lead in it. So we was laughing 'cause the war was over and we was still living and death was through fucking with us. And then we got up to walk into Charbonne and Vashtey stepped on a mine and blew his nuts up into his throat and even before he asked me to, I shot him in the head. And I knew him well. Nothing personal, home-boy, but you don't want to come over here with that.

(Beat)

BENNET: Mister Clifford set a date for your grandmother's funeral?

CHI-TOWN: A funeral? Now that's a nice idea. 'Cause, see, I thought that's what they do for you when you fall out, washing somebody's toilet and you too damn tired to get up. They digs a hole and puts you in it, 'stead'a

letting you go rotten for a week or two in George
Clifford's basement.

HAROLD: I cain't take this. I already got high pressure
and my sugar been bad! Negroes getting shot up and
stabbed up and everyone of yaw come back from
overseas complete fools. I'm moving to Baltimore,
live with my sister.

SYLVESTER: What your sister look like, Harold?

HAROLD: Don't start with me, Sylvester Roy.

SYLVESTER: *(Slams down another bone)* Give me fifteen.

(Door opens, SHERIFF FRANK *steps in the door, stops short of
the blood, then steps over it. Conversation stops.* NATE *drops
the newspaper and quickly exits. Only* SYLVESTER *is looking
at* FRANK.*)*

FRANK: That boy ain't never been quite right, has he,
Sylvester? *(Beat)* Well, all these years we been knowing
each other, Sylvester Roy, and this here's my first time
I been in Willy's Cut and Shine! And you know what,
I been meaning to ask you, who in the hell is Willy?

SYLVESTER: Give me ten. Willy Sampson. Come back
from the first big war, had the good sense to leave,
went to Kansas, believe his wife had family there.

FRANK: Kansas? Now Durham ain't too bad once't you
get know it. Bennet went up North for all that schooling
and couldn't wait to get back! Ain't that right?

BENNET: Couldn't wait.

FRANK: Cold as a witches tit, ain't it? Ain't seen weather
like this since '32. You remember '32, Sylvester Roy?
(Silence) I said, you remember...

SYLVESTER: *(Slaps bone down hard, they jump up off the
table.)* '32 was bad. Whatn't bad as this. *(Writing down
the score)* Give me fifteen!

HAROLD: *(Looking over his shoulder at* FRANK*)* You got the pad.

FRANK: *(Having a hard time taking his eyes off the blood stain on the floor)* Things like this...like this are...that stain ain't come up too good. *(Pause. Pushing his hat through his hands)* Wanted to give you a couple days to get through the burying 'fore I...

SYLVESTER: You early. Grounds too hard.

FRANK: Grounds too hard? We buried ol' man Stromsen three days ago.

SYLVESTER: White folk get buried on high ground. Negroes is buried in the wet lands. You know that. Been that way since we was in short pants. Won't stay down in the summer, won't go down in the winter. Summer of '93 was bad. You 'member summer '93 don't you?

FRANK: I remember '93. I don't recall no stories about dead folk rising.

SYLVESTER: Don't you? Bad summer for sugar cane and Negroes. *(Slams bone down hard)* Give me ten. We cut down more Negroes than cane that year. *(Slams another bone down hard)* Matter fact, Stromsen was mayor then, whatn't he? *(Slams another bone down hard)* Had hisself a good laugh. "Cain't nobody say we keeps the Nigra down in Durham County. Everytime you turn around one is coming up!" We was coming up quicker than we was going down, and for a Negro in Georgia, that ain't easy!

(Small laughter all around except FRANK.*)*

FRANK: Seem like you'd appreciate the fact nobody had to cut you out a tree, Sylvester.

*(*SYLVESTER *slams a bone down.)*

FRANK: Well this ain't quite the time to reminisce, is it? Thought I might find Quincey here. I drove all the way out to that a...you seen the shack he's living in out there, look like who did Sally and what for...all that property his brother had...

CLAUDE: Had?

FRANK: You know where Quincey is, Sylvester?

SYLVESTER: None of my business where Quincey's keep hisself.

FRANK: Maybe you oughtta make it your business, Sylvester Roy! In the midst of all his grief, if he stumbles in the wrong place, it's gonna be your business!

CLAUDE: *(Still looking at the paper)* I'm surprised you found time to stop by at all, Sheriff. All this business, then you got the whole county to worry 'bout. Must keep you busy.

FRANK: *(Perturbed)* I reckon so.

CLAUDE: Yes suh, must be tough, Sheriffing-keeping the peace, making the crooked way straight, with business like this. I mean ain't that why you drove all the way through uptown, all the way down here to the Bottom, brought yourself up in Willy's Cut and Shine for "good Lord Sylvester Roy the first time," to make the crooked way straight?

FRANK: I didn't come here to discuss my job requirements.

CLAUDE: Oh you ain't got to come in here and discuss the law! I just finished ducking and dodging bullets for the law, I know all about the law...

SYLVESTER: Claude...

CLAUDE: ...the law say if you walking 'cross the street and somebody take a shotgun and open up your chest...

SYLVESTER: Claude!

CLAUDE: ...the law say they supposed to pay something, last time I checked that's what the law say!

FRANK: Last time I checked, Colored kept their place in Durham proper and I don't expect no changes, no time soon!

CHI-TOWN: Whew! That's the end of that, ain't it?

HAROLD: (*Lays a bone down soft*) I'll take that ten.

FRANK: How long you was in that war, boy?

CLAUDE: Boy? You don't look nothing like my daddy.

FRANK: I said how long you was in that war?!

CLAUDE: Day after they said we was in it.

FRANK: We? You was gone a good while. Maybe you forgot how this work.

CLAUDE: Whatn't gone that long.

FRANK: Then you know I don't make the rules but I make the rules work, *that's* what the law does! Hell, some days I wish things was a bit different. But they ain't. This is the way the world is made and everybody got a place in it! Even me, I got a place. Know your place, learn when to cut your loses, you might live to be an old man. You look up in the tree and it ain't you. Itn't that right, Sylvester?

(SYLVESTER *does not look up, slams bone down hard and they all jump off the table again.*)

FRANK: Now, I'm not happy about what happened to Louis....

CLAUDE: You not happy?

FRANK: Louis went too far, Sylvester, and you know that.

CLAUDE: (*Looking to everyone in the shop*) He act like he standing in spilt milk!

FRANK: Sylvester Roy...

CLAUDE: That's blood, that's what he had left....

FRANK: Sylvester!

CLAUDE: ...cause a shotgun don't leave a lot of nothing!

FRANK: ...you better talk to this boy!

(SYLVESTER *slams a bone down on the table.*)

HAROLD: Damn, Syl.

FRANK: You think people in this town are stupid? Louis living in that big house of his? Clothes come with postage from France. Ordering masonry and tile out'a Italy. Hell anybody living like that might forget their place in the world. Ain't that right, Syl? But you cain't keep pushing on people like that, they liable to push back. (*Pushing his hat through his hands*) Tuck Wilmot is coming here, tomorrow noon. Louis secured all that mess he ordered with his properties, his businesses and....

CLAUDE: You standing in his business!

FRANK: Tuck is coming here tomorrow and I'm coming with him. I'm telling you right now, Sylvester Roy, I'll shoot the first dog that barks. The Wilmot's got legal papers.

CLAUDE: Naw. The Wilmots got you, the good Sheriff Frank.

FRANK: You boys come back from overseas, sipping out of pretty cups across the table from pretty women and you think the whole world done changed. Nothing changed. Georgia still Georgia. You ain't done nothing over there that'll keep you from swinging at the end of fresh Georgia twine off the some of the prettiest oak

trees on God's green earth. *(Puts on hat to leave)*
You remember when we were kids, Sylvester?
The young bulls in the fields start acting the fool,
first thing to go, the balls. Calmed'em right down didn't
it? I'd make sure and keep a lid on this if I were you.
Now is the time to be smart. Be a shame to live this
long, not learn nothing. *(He steps over the blood spot.)*
You see Quincey, you need to have a word with him.
Tomorrow noon... Seem like a little lye and a brush get
this right up.

BENNET: Yes, certainly does seem like it would.

(FRANK exits.)

SYLVESTER: *(Writing it down)* Would you hurry up and
play that funky six-one you been holding since '42.

BENNET: Maybe we should just wait. I can't believe
Louis would sign over a single piece property to...

CLAUDE: *(Pointing to the blood spot)* What kind of
paperwork do he really need, Bennet?

CHI-TOWN: How 'bout that next game, old man?
Two out of three.

CLAUDE: You need to go on back over to Simpsons,
see if you cain't get up a game.

CHI-TOWN: *(Pointing at the blood spot)* Hell, look like
come tomorrow, little after noon, all yaw be over to
Simpson's trying to get up a game.

CLAUDE: I tol' you to go somewhere.

CHI-TOWN: I know it ain't easy for you, I mean, after all,
you the cat put a bullet in your ace boon coon's head,
ain't you? And here the good Sheriff come in through
and punked you out! You Negroes talk all that mess
'bout what you did, what you gonna do... sound like
you was standing in the window, ain't did shit, ain't
about to do shit!

(CLAUDE *turns to come across the room for* CHI-TOWN, *grabs him by the chest and hems him up against the wall.* BENNET *and* HAROLD *pull* CLAUDE *off* CHI-TOWN.)

SYLVESTER: Good Lord, boy, you trying to get kilt?

CHI-TOWN: *(Breathing hard, he gets to his feet.)* I come in for a game. Make a couple dollars cause that's what I do! *(Smashes his fist on the table)* I don't do nothing but take yo' money! Least with me you come back tomorrow, try yo' luck again but naw, you wanna put me in a box! Everyday you old ass Negroes look at yo'self in the mirror and you cain't stand it, can you! I look at you coming down the street and I cain't stand it! Cain't do shit! You cain't even bury nobody's grandma, she laying up going rotten and she ain't never been nothing but good! You hear me, but now, bossman come through and all the sudden yo' feet stuck to the floor but you wanna put me in a box!

CLAUDE: I ain't run half way 'cross the world for your...

CHI-TOWN: *(Arms stretched wide, laughing and wiping blood on his shirt)* You ain't took one step 'cross the world I'm living in! You ain't done nothing for me!

CLAUDE: *(Throws some money on the floor)* That's what you need, ain't it? Take a hit, take a train. Take it and go on 'bout your business. You don't know nothing about this.

CHI-TOWN: *(Stares at the money, sniffling, wiping his nose.)* I know it back to front, Home-boy! What it is, what it ain't, what it's gonna be 'cause it don't never change! 'Cept tomorrow noon, this be a shell, then what you gone do! Bunch a'homeless Negroes standing in the street and I'm supposed to be impressed 'bout how you operating in the world? I take a hit cause I need it and when I step out into my world, baby! it's big! Way bigger than this! *(Picking up the money, or not, is a choice.*

Starts to exit, stops at the LOUIS *blood spot.)* But you gone see me 'fore I go. Bet you gone see me.

(Exits quickly, NATE *enters, looking after* CHI-TOWN *as he closes the door.* CLAUDE *moves to get his coat.)*

SYLVESTER: Where you going. Claude?

CLAUDE: *(Has his coat on)* Don't you wanna know, just once, what it feels like to own the little bit of space you occupy in the world? Not to be shuffling down the street looking at yo' shoes for no damn reason?

SYLVESTER: Louis took up all the space he stood in and the ground won't even open up for him. I'm telling you this is the way the world work.

CLAUDE: I'm sorry for what you been through, cutting all them men outta them trees. I'm sorry time done put this on us, but something got to be done wit' it. Bible say let the dead take care of the dead, and we ain't dead. I told you, I ain't waiting on you or Quincey or nobody else. *(He exits.)*

HAROLD: He's crazy as a betsy bug. His daddy was crazy, both his uncles was crazy, you 'member Dutch? Crazy as a betsy bug.

NATE: I just went by Georges. Everything was real quiet.

(They all stop to look at NATE.*)*

SYLVESTER: It's a funeral home, Nate. Dead folk don't make much noise.

NATE: I'm telling you it's so quiet, you cain't hear nothing else.

HAROLD: Please, Nate.

NATE: You go by Georges, you'll see. It's so quiet till you cain't hear nothing else.

SYLVESTER: Simple.

BENNET: Pray tell, what does the quiet sound like, Mister Nate?

NATE: Crying. Sound like a whole bunch of folk crying.

(The sound of an engine gunning by outside. Everyone is stock still in the after moment of silence. SYLVESTER rises and puts on his coat.)

HAROLD: Where you going?

SYLVESTER: Go home, Harold. You lucky Helen still waiting on you to show up everyday. Bennet.

BENNET: Mister Sylvester.

(SYLVESTER exits.)

HAROLD: *(He rises to put his coat on.)* I swear I'm moving to Baltimore. You gone be here in the morning, Bennet?

BENNET: That's my job till it isn't, Mister Harold.

(HAROLD exits. NATE picks up the paper and sits in a barber's chair.)

NATE: Seem like everybody trying to go somewhere.

BENNET: Tuck Wilmot will be here tomorrow, stroke of noon. Says he hold the paper to everything Louis owned, including Willy's Cut and Shine.

NATE: That mean....

BENNET: I don't know what that means.

NATE: I don't like the chairs at Simpsons, and then he ain't never got enough, you got to stand around till somebody...

BENNET: Mister Nate. I believe this is the end of the day.

NATE: What you gone do, Bennet? You going back up North?

BENNET: Cross that bridge when I get to it.

NATE: Kind of look like we at it.

(NATE *exits.* BENNET *takes off his smock and exits. Moments later* QUINCEY *enters, stares at the blood spot for a moment, then sits on the mourner's bench. Black out)*

END OF ACT ONE

ACT TWO

(Fade up dim. QUINCEY *sits up in the empty barber shop, transfixed for a moment on the blood. Gets a mop and bucket and scrubs furiously for a moment then throws the mop and bucket across the space. The sound of ocean waves crashing on the side of a ship stops him.* CAPTAIN, *pipe in hand, staunch uniform enters into spotlight upstage. The sound of a long foghorn sounds in the distance.* LOLAR *enters from stage right and sets up a portable stool, meticulously packing his shoulder sack. There are the requisite items, K-rations, knife, socks, condoms, underwear, a packet of pictures and letters, two small books and boots.* LOLAR *is smiling, going home.* QUINCEY *moves down to* LOLAR.)

CAPTAIN: *(Spotlight up on* CAPTAIN, *booming, turning downstage.)* We're going home boys! We been through it, I know, but if this oversized excuse of a ship holds back the ocean another few days! we're going home!

(Spotlight off, he measures his movement across stage and is still.)

LOLAR: *(Wiggling fingers and toes, laughing)* We got all our shit, huh? Ten fingers, ten toes, good bladder, liver, everything working. Going home.

CAPTAIN: See here, I need a word with you all. I say, just take a moment, but I need to have a word...

QUINCEY: That's how it feel, don't it? Feel like you come in the world with everything you need...

CAPTAIN: ...Quincey! We laid'em low, didn't we?

QUINCEY: Captain, my Captain.

CAPTAIN: I thought we left you in France! Did you hear anything I...

QUINCEY: I come home, for Louis.

LOLAR: You ever been to Harlem, Q'?

QUINCEY: Ain't been nowhere...come to see 'bout Louis...

LOLAR: I hear they throws a ton of tore up paper from the windows and...!

QUINCEY: Got a country in his chest so big, dirt won't fill it, I cain't fill it!

LOLAR: ...and women? Redbones! from blackberry to peaches, so thick and ripe they pressing the vine...

CAPTAIN: You think I can't look you in the eye when I say this? With all we've been through? I'm looking you in the eye!

QUINCEY: Louis come in the world shining like brand new money...I held him in all that blood and mess, one'a my Aunt stretched the cord tight and I cut it!

LOLAR: Peaches! I'm gone sink my teeth through all that meat, right down to the seed...

QUINCEY: I did everything I was supposed to do....

CAPTAIN: You think I don't know what you did? I laid in the mud and laid men low with you!

LOLAR: ...and juice, thick as blood, gone fly!

CAPTAIN: You and me, through Germany and Italy and France like a hurricane! I wasn't pushing papers or driving some four star from countryside to countryside. I was right there with you!

QUINCEY: I say, shhhhh, quiet now...quiet.

LOLAR: They gone be lined up, Q', from here to Harlem, and we gone run....

QUINCEY: I done all the running I'm gone do! My feets bad and I'm tired! You hear me say I'm tired?

LOLAR: You got the whole eternity to be looking up at wood and dirt, angels singing that mess so sweet you cain't stand it. I know that's what you pray for every night! But right now, they's blackberrys and peaches lined up from here to Harlem just waiting....

CAPTAIN: *(Spotlight up on* CAPTAIN *again as he turns downstage, pipe in hand.)* No, no, no! Do you really want to know what they've thought up these days back home? I'll tell you the truth, because we put aside all the mess that means nothing between soldiers and walked through life and death together, saw good men come and go together! *(Beat)* Before the war? That was nothing.

(Spotlight out)

QUINCEY: You see? You don't know what I come home to. Your piece back puzzle ass got Harlem everyday but I come home where everything is tied down to the earth, ain't nobody waiting, no arms open wide to wrap you in the sweetest shit since mother's milk, no parades and ticker tape streaming, no room on the train where you get on naw you got to walk yo' ass cross a whole 'nother country, 'cross a whole 'nother Germany and they sitting there grinning with teeth big as harvest moons, watching you walk by on your way to that country of seats in the back and they look like-ain't it good to be home!.... They done cracked fifteen picks and the ground is hard as the first rock God ever spit up and Louis still won't go down...the *ground* won't even take you!

CAPTAIN: *(Spotlight up, paces back and forth now)* What are they doing? What are they doing? You really want to know? Lets see, they're lynching, yep, that's an old standby and then they're burning them out, drowning them out, shooting them out, lets see, what else is there oh yes there's the cutting, oh that's the worst, then of course they have to cut off the the the you know because they could always come back as ghost and FUCK our women yes yes yes that's it...fuck our women. *(Stops stock still. Almost gayly now.)* That's what they're doing these days. *(Spotlight out.)*

QUINCEY: I'm telling you, the ground won't even take you.

LOLAR: You wanna be clean...

QUINCEY: Cooper...

LOLAR: ...good bladder...

QUINCEY: ...washing up like...

LOLAR: ...good liver...

QUINCEY: ...washing up like driftwood...

LOLAR: ...arms and legs...

QUINCEY: ...nothing but washed up k-rats!

LOLAR: *(Crying.)* That Negro washed up loaded with peach cobbler and I got full! I still got some!

QUINCEY: Bunch a field niggas! Only we whatn't picking cotton or tobacco or beans, naw...we's harvesting democracy, yas suh boss! I pick a kraut off the vine for yah!....you put yo' bushel on the back of the truck and you don't get shit!

CAPTAIN: *(Spotlight up, holding the pipe, turns downstage nonchalant)* You could stay, indeed you could, right here in France. They love your dusky, primitive, rough, romantic antics here. It is good to be loved, isn't it, needed, respected, cared for. Indeed. Indeed.

(Spotlight out.)

QUINCEY: Skin like milk...

LOLAR: *(Pushes the .45 into* QUINCEY'*s hand)* Feel that.
Feel good, right? That's real. Like a good woman feel
in yo' hands. Huh? Deloqua!

QUINCEY: Like when you make the cream rise

LOLAR: That's real, ain't it?

QUINCEY: I seen it. Seven years old and I seen it all.
Seen ol' man Wilmot take my mama, in the pantry,
in the kitchen, the back hallway, outside the house
in the middle of a rainstorm!

LOLAR: Great day in the morning I cain't wait to get
home!

QUINCEY: Everyday, everyday she say, shhh, quiet now
Quincey, shhhh...quiet now...we got to live the best we
can. But I *seen* it, didn't I?

CAPTAIN: You can't take nothing home with you!

LOLAR: You seen me come out that ditch!

CAPTAIN: I just want to see you stay above ground....

QUINCEY: Skin that was just skin....

LOLAR: You seen me fly, thick as blood you seen me fly!

QUINCEY: Skin waiting on me.

CAPTAIN: ....all we been through I just want to see you
stay above ground for a while.

LOLAR: Come out wit' me this time.

CAPTAIN: You go home the way you came. You hear
me, just the way you came! That's the way it is!

QUINCEY: Skin waiting on me!

LOLAR: Right above the nose! That's how we did it,
right Q? I don't say that right between eyes shit cause it
sound like you whatn't really there like you was in yo'

back yard looking at some kids 'cross the fence and you
ain't really seen shit....

QUINCEY: I seen it...

LOLAR: That's why we sitting here scraping salt spray
off our ass, we kept our shit clean and planted Krauts
with boots cleaner than the ones you could polish till
kingdom come and never get right planted 'em-BLAM-
and maybe some of the brothers we left over there
got planted like you plant a tree only a tree is coming
up better than it went in and maybe them brothers is
coming up better than they went in but for damn sure
you cain't plant shit in this weather!

CAPTAIN: (*Spotlight up, laughing to point of crying.*)
You don't get any of the pie! None of it! Don't ask
me why! (*Abruptly*) I know what you did! You think
I wasn't there? I was there.

LOLAR: I'm washed in the blood...

QUINCEY: Baptized in the fire...

LOLAR: Bible say you walk out the other side of that...

QUINCEY: You brand new!

LOLAR: Louis ain't going down in this weather!

CAPTAIN: I'm telling you, Quincey, you don't give that
up, you go home to a whole new war.

QUINCEY: I gave! You think 'cause I'm sitting here,
'cause Lolar and Cooper ain't sitting here, I ain't gave
nothing?!

CAPTAIN: (*He turns in the spotlight and looks to heaven.*)
What do you want from me?!

QUINCEY: Nothing. Seem like there was a time, deep in
the past-time wanna-be's of a child, when anything was
possible...you tell yourself, when you grown, you can
be what you come in the world to be...but in the muck

and mire you lose yo' way till one day it come back to you...I come in the world with everything I need.

CAPTAIN: *(Quietly)* I'm sorry, but you don't get none of the pie, you hear me, none.

LOLAR: Where there's two, come together in my name....

CAPTAIN: *(From the shadows, again)* It's time to go home, boys.

QUINCEY: Piece a thunder like this...

CAPTAIN: *(From the shadows, talking up stage)* It's time to go home.

LOLAR: We get hold to one them peaches, Q, sink our teeth all the way down to the seed and juice, thick as blood, will fly. "You better come on in my kitchen 'cause it's going to be raining outdoors, said, it's going to be raining outdoors."

(LOLAR exits, jubilant. CAPTAIN exits, weary.)

LOLAR: We gone do some damage up in Harlem, ain't we Q!

QUINCEY: He's coming, Mama, Louis, he be there soon...man do what he wanna do with' his life, ain't no shame in dying, living like you wanna live.... You know I'm tired, right? I'm tired in my bones, Mama, but I'm gone make a way...and Louis, he be there soon...and when he get there, don't turn around, Mama, I gone be right behind him...

(QUINCEY sits and takes all the shoe shining gear out of his pocket and lays it on the floor, takes off his boots and sock, whispering in his bare feet he picks up the .45, exits. Lights fade. BENNET enters singing carrying a newspaper and book under his arm, a small sack and a thermos. He stops short of the blood spot before stepping over it and placing his items on the card table, then hangs coat and hat. He takes sandwich and tea bag out of his sack, opens thermos and pours water

over the tea bag, sits in the barber chair with cup and sandwich, hovers over the first bite, looking at the blood spot. Sees the gear QUINCEY *left behind. He places it all up stage, brings a bucket and brush back down to the blood. There is a knock at the door. Stops dead still, pause, another knock, stronger.)*

BENNET: *(From his knees)* We are closed. *(Another knock. Rising now)* I said, we are closed!

CLAUDE: It's Claude, Bennet.

(Pause. Unlocks and opens the door for CLAUDE. CLAUDE *enters laughing, carrying his own sack and thermos, stepping wide over the blood spot.)*

CLAUDE: Big day.

BENNET: Indeed. Noon. I thought I might wake up to a bonfire this morning.

CLAUDE: Sometimes you kind's funny, Bennet. And sometimes...

BENNET: I understand. Listen, I come for the momentary peace and calm. Depending upon Mister Wilmot's...well I may not have this opportunity tomorrow. Between my mother, her pekeno friends, I need a quiet moment. Just me, my tea, and a good book.

*(*CLAUDE *is busy in his own sack.)*

BENNET: Not too many people out this time of the morning. Nothing personal, but it's my strong desire you have somewhere else to be this morning.

CLAUDE: It is kind of quiet, ain't it?

BENNET: It was.

(Both men laugh.)

CLAUDE: I know what you mean. Quiet spot. Man don't know what that's worth 'till he look up and ain't

nothing but noise. Right? Nothing but noise.
(Offers up his thermos) Coffee?

BENNET: *(Holds up his own cup)* Tea.

CLAUDE: *(Walking to the window)* Yeah. You, me,
and Johnson's mama.

BENNET: You saw her this morning?

CLAUDE: Sitting on Simpson's porch, she scared the
shit out of me.

BENNET: Simpson tells me she comes every day, but this
is a bit early. Simpson says she buys a beer and two
aspirin every time she comes through. She says the
beer is for the headache and the aspirin is for the beer!
(Both men laugh light and tight.) You've been by to see
her since you got back?

CLAUDE: *(Continually looking out the window)* What I'm
going by there for?

BENNET: Maybe she just wants to hear how he stood up
and...

CLAUDE: Yeah, she sitting on Simpson's front porch at
six in the morning 'cause she wanna know how her
boy stood up. Don't take no degree to know what she
wants, what a whole bunch of mothers want. *(Puts his
hand out on an imaginary chest and feels it rising and
falling)* She wants to put her hand on her boy's chest
and feel it rising and falling. That's what I used to do.
The young brothers laid out. They eyes be this big.
(Hands stretched wide) They be missing all kinds of arms
and legs and asses and I put my hands on they chest
and tell'em, look here. Grab a handful of hair if I had
to so they could see. They see they own shit rising and
falling and for that half a second, they got everything
they need. That's what she wants. Whatn't nothing left
for me to put my hands on. I hear they give her a little

letter and a funky flag for her trouble. My grandmother used to say some rocks is better left lying in the river.

BENNET: What a wonderful idiom. No doubt from a paragon of wisdom and a sentiment that I'm sure is widely held by many Negroes. It's a pity more folk don't take her advice, more often.

CLAUDE: Ain't it though. *(Pause)* Tea. Maybe I should do tea. Seem like everyday now my stomach is all up in knots. I used to keep a little reefer growing in my back yard 'fore the war...

BENNET: What are you doing, Claude? This time of the morning?

CLAUDE: Hauling grain up to Marysville. I want to get it done, out the way.

BENNET: What is that, about an hour, with a stop to smell the roses? Forty minutes otherwise?

CLAUDE: Ain't no roses on the way to Marysville.

BENNET: I believe that's my point.

CLAUDE: Come with me, Bennet.

BENNET: I've been to Marysville.

CLAUDE: You know what I'm talking 'bout.

BENNET: Nothing I need from Wilmot's hardware. Nothing you need either.

CLAUDE: I need to go in there, put something down on Tuck, I wanna see the same look on his face Louis had, that look we all seen standing at that window.

BENNET: Claude, you realize how close to the mouth of hell we are teetering? You have a conkhead junkie from Chicago who wants to stick something, anything sharp he can put his hands on, in your ass. Tuck Wilmont will be here in *(Looks at his watch.)* six, seven hours to buy, steal, or simply take the property of the man we all seen

him casually murder. Why? Because he can. Louis has
been lying in a funeral parlor all ready half a week.
Why? Well he had the misfortune to be young,
intelligent, wealthy, and black all at the same time in
Durham, Georgia during the coldest winter since 1932.
Not to mention we have no idea what Quincey will do
when he gets here. And in the midst of all of this-you
come in here, disturb my peace to say, come haul some
grain to Marysville with me!

CLAUDE: You think that door is keeping out the world?
World be here noon today. You got all that shit up in
your head and you in here, killing time.

BENNET: *(Smiling)* An innocent murder.

CLAUDE: No such thing, Bennet. *(Walks to the window)*
We do this and whatever ran you up in here, won't
mean nothing.

BENNET: Nothing ran me...

CLAUDE: *(Whirling, laughing)* Six weeks after we left out
of here we was on that ocean. Told us we was going to
France. You step up on deck, ain't nothing but water
everywhere you turn. Third day out a storm come up
and them waves was coming ass high to cotton and big
as that ship was, Mother nature was whomping its ass.
We go down with one of them waves and a wall of
water all around, ride it to the top and you could see
horizon everywhere. Negroes was sweating, you hear
me! Vashtey say, "This rock sink, what you gone do?"
I say, "Swim, Negro. What you gone do?" He say,
"Which way you gone swim?" I say, "Hell, it really
don't matter which way. The whole world at war."
He say, "We in the middle of this damn ocean with the
waves rocking this boat like juke joint Sally, and you
mean to tell me, yo' ass gonna swim all the way back
to Georgia?" I say, "You ain't got but two choices, Vash,

sink or swim." He say, "Hell, I cain't swim for shit but you ain't leaving me out here."

BENNET: That's a nice story but...

CLAUDE: I put a bullet in Vashtey's head. I got to do something with that, I cain't leave him out there like that.

BENNET: The man say it ain't your brother.

CLAUDE: Vashtey's due! I'm due, Bennet.

BENNET: Everybody's due! Everybody ought to get more than they got, live better than what came before.

CLAUDE: Bible say the middle ground ain't worth spit.

BENNET: Oh, now, I am surprised!

CLAUDE: *(Smiling)* You think I don't know God?

BENNET: The important question is whether or not God knows you! Whether God in his infinite wisdom will look down from his high place today and say, turn about is fair play, let the dusky sons of Ethiop participate in the community of men. Whether today is the day he says, "Well done my good and faithful servant. You have swung from enough sycamores, lay at the bottom of enough oceans, taken the bit and bore the lash enough for ten generations—the price is well paid, get the hell out of Egyptland and sup your days away in peace." That is the question, Mister Claude. Does he know who the hell you are, because he's been awful quiet for, oh, I don't know, what? A few hundred years now?

CLAUDE: I'm not waiting on God. I'm not gonna sit here like Harold and Sylvester hoping nobody finds out my whole life is a game of dominoes. You know what I'm saying Bennet. You know.....

BENNET: You heard Sylvester. What I know ain't doing nothing for me! I'm doing what I came to do. I cut

heads. I look after my mama. I don't owe you or
nobody else.

CLAUDE: Everybody pays. The only question is,
you get your money's worth?

BENNET: I'm satisfied.

CLAUDE: How the hell you satisfied? I know you ain't
talking 'bout this? Willy's Cut and Shine? We don't do
this, Tuck Wilmont be here noon to take this. *(Points at
the blood spot on the floor)* Look at this shit and tell me
how satisfied you are.

BENNET: *(Tight)* That's a bucket. A bit of water. And a
brush.

CLAUDE: *(Now at the window, his head in his palms.)* We
seen it, didn't we, standing right here. Five grown men.
We stood here and watched Tuck Wilmot shoot Louis
down and leave him like trash in the street. We stood
right here and watched him drive away like it was
Sunday morning and then, then we brought him in here
so at least he finish bleeding to death on something
familiar! Every day, Bennet. We cain't say we ain't
seen it! You got a bucket and a brush for that, Bennet?
(He finishes his coffee in one swig, recaps his thermos.)

BENNET: *(Looking at his hands)* Boston. That's where I
was. But it wasn't about-Boston. I thought once I got
that piece of paper it could take me where my skin
couldn't. I used to see hundreds of Mister Sylvesters on
my way to the train station. And I thought, never me. I
know the secret, I know the code. Have you ever seen a
University degree, Claude? Sheepskin, inlaid gold leafs
around the edges, letters in these huge, flourished
strokes. I put it behind glass and mahogany, hung it at
the foot of my bed so that I could see her reflection in
it whenever she sat up on me and how unbelievably
fine the light brown of her back was, mixed with that
mahogany and gold, and weeks later after I went

everywhere and got nowhere and doors kept shutting before I even got to them in the great North, the great land of equality, milk and honey—I was not the least bit amazed that I couldn't see her reflection because of this—pinkish looking man who was riding above her, he looked like some kind of boat on a light brown ocean. It was a long day, my skin was tired and from the doorway I could barely see flashes of her underneath him so I stepped into the room and for a moment I thought I was hoping maybe she wasn't really there. But she was. I was so surprised I stood absolutely still while he beat me nearly to death and that, Claude, is why I am here cutting heads and dispensing philosophy. What I know ain't doing nothing for me.

CLAUDE: *(He packs his mess up and slips on his coat to leave.)* After today, won't be no room in the middle.

(He is at the door when BENNET *speaks. He does not turn around)*

BENNET: Claude. You want a cut before you go?

CLAUDE: I look like I need a cut?

BENNET: *(Smiling)* You know they don't allow no combs in jail.

(Pause. They are eye to eye for a moment.)

CLAUDE: Jail?

*(*CLAUDE *laughs, exits.* BENNET *wraps his uneaten sandwich and puts it back in the paper bag, begins to lay out his barber gear. Lights fade up full on the shop as the patrons enter,* NATE, SYLVESTER, *and* HAROLD. NATE *sits in the unused barber chair, reading the paper.* SYLVESTER *and* HAROLD *are both at their regular spots at the card table, dominoes in hand, in the midst of the unending game. It is a small piece of time before* SYLVESTER *speaks.)*

SYLVESTER: Jesus, Harold-would you play the bone!

HAROLD: Is them Quincey's boots? They look like Quincey's boots. You know he don't go nowhere without them boots on his feet or in his hands.

(Everyone ignores HAROLD.*)*

SYLVESTER: Today is like any other day we ever come in here.

HAROLD: Ain't nothing about today like any other day.

NATE: Louis lost that fight with Marciano and retired.

SYLVESTER: *(Pause)* What I tell you?

NATE: Knocked him out in the eighth.

SYLVESTER: Play the six-one.

HAROLD: *(Irritated)* Would you for once stay out of my hand? That's the only thing ain't never changed around here.

SYLVESTER: You always got the six-one, Harold. You always slow as molasses on a oak tree in January and you always got the six-one.

HAROLD: *(Lays down the six-one.)* Anything else I can do for you?

SYLVESTER: *(He slams down his bone.)* You can give me fifteen.

HAROLD: *(Staring at the boots)* You got the pad. Bennet, you see Quincey this morning?

BENNET: No.

SYLVESTER: Claude been here?

BENNET: No.

HAROLD: I should'a stayed in bed. Anybody know what time it is?

SYLVESTER: Damn, Harold! Noon be here when it get here.

BENNET: So will Quincey or Claude, Mister Sylvester. Be here when they get here.

NATE: Had to cut both eyes for they stopped it.

(The sound of an engine gunning by and SYLVESTER *and* HAROLD *and* BENNET *lean into the sound, waiting. In the aftermath, a beat.)*

NATE: You know how much money Louis made on that fight? One hundred twenty three thousand two hundred fifty-six dollars and thirty-five cent.

SYLVESTER: Louis ain't made no one hundred and...

NATE: Says it right here.

SYLVESTER: *(Lays down a bone.)* Joe Louis the only Colored man in America, hell, the world! who can legally whoop a White man's ass, which he did regular for a while, and you think they gone let him have the money too! Paper liable to say anything. *(Slams down a bone)*

BENNET: It's common knowledge that Joe Louis is doing well for himself. Everybody in the civilized world know Joe living in the fat. But that's just a bit too much for you to take to take, Colored man doing well. Fact of the matter is...

SYLVESTER: *Facts* is what you talk about when the dust clears. *Facts* say the last place you supposed to be right now is behind that chair.

HAROLD: All right, Syl. Play your bone.

SYLVESTER: Facts say you supposed to be up in some fancy school in New York or Boston or Baltimore, talking 'bout how facts run the world! First time somebody steps you off a sidewalk Uptown, without even saying a word, facts don't mean shit. Do they, Mister Bennet?

BENNET: What I come home for is my business.

HAROLD: *(Quickly coming in)* Play the bone, Syl?

SYLVESTER: How you think that work, Harold?

HAROLD: The man say stay out his business.

SYLVESTER: I ain't getting in the man's business. I'm just asking how you think that work.

HAROLD: I wouldn't know.

SYLVESTER: Hell, ain't many people would. You go off to school, went big ticket. School putting out presidents and folks running the country! And here you is cutting heads. Talk like you got encyclopedias spilling out yo' ass and here you is cutting heads! Matter fact, when you come back you looking like three, fo' miles of bad road and yo' mama got to foot the bill for...

BENNET: *(Hot)* My mother never put out a dime for me!

SYLVESTER: And here he is telling us how facts make the world go 'round! I ain't getting in the man's business. I'm just asking, how you think that work!

BENNET: What can I tell you that you don't already know, Mister Sylvester? Or should I say, that you haven't seen. I imagine one can see the whole world from a moving train.

(Beat)

HAROLD: *(He slams a bone down.)* I'm going to Baltimore.

NATE: Say here Joe Louis got a restaurant in Detroit.

HAROLD: *(The dominoes are moving now, HAROLD throws one down right after the other, SYLVESTER can barely keep up.)* My sister say they got houses, run the whole block.

NATE: Got a farm in Springfield.

HAROLD: *(Slams down another bone)* They got trolleys running right outside the front door....

NATE: A duece and a quarter he give his sister.

HAROLD: You jump it while it's running.... *(Lays down another bone)* ...drop you right at the corner grocer.

NATE: Put his sister through Howard, paid every dime.

HAROLD: *(Slams another bone down)* I'm going to Baltimore. *(Doesn't wait for* SYLVESTER, *and slams another)* I ain't packing shit. *(Slams another)* I ain't taking shit. *(Slams another)* And don't call me!

BENNET: The world is coming, isn't it? That's what Claude said this morning.

SYLVESTER: Claude was here?

BENNET: I should have had the coffee. Soon as he opened the lid you could smell how strong it was.

SYLVESTER: I thought you said you ain't seen Claude.

BENNET: That's what you need on a day like today, Mister Sylvester, strong black coffee. Not tea.

SYLVESTER: What we need to do is finish this game 'fore noon get....

BENNET: Wake up Mister Sylvester! You didn't hear Mister Harold? Ain't nothing about today like any other day, but you think Tuck Wilmot is gonna make it here today?

SYLVESTER: I been beating Harold at the same game for thirty years.

BENNET: You wanna believe Joe Louis ain't got a dime to his name but you think Tuck Wilmot is showing up here today!

SYLVESTER: *(Lays a bone down)* Give me ten.

BENNET: Carrie—I tell you about Carrie? She whatn't
big on coffee. Black olives. Three o'clock in the morning
and we'd be standing at the box, eating black olives,
this big! I tell you, one bite, and your heart breaks.
Black juice flies from your mouth and salt, deep as
any ocean, attacks your tongue, and you will love
somebody, trust me. You cannot prevent it.

SYLVESTER: *(Distracted)* Play the...play the...play the
two-three.

HAROLD: You think I'm sitting here for you

BENNET: And then there was Sunday mornings, the
Sunday paper. It's that thick. You remember? No.
Of course you wouldn't remember. First you'd have
to want the paper. Then you'd have to actually get off
the train, find a news stand...

SYLVESTER: *(Lays down a bone)* Give me five.

BENNET: I would run to the market, early, right before
sunrise. Even then, I never really left her. After olives
at three how could I. I was tethered to her ankle,
this invisible line that ran from her ankle to my chest.
And we would spend the entire day with the paper,
everywhere. Once, we made love on the crossword
puzzle then smoothed it out later and did it together.
That's the only crossword puzzle I ever finished.
And it was the same as the olives and the making
love and everything else we did that morning.

SYLVESTER: You hear this mess, Harold. Ranches in
Springfield and Sunday papers and black olives. What!
What do I give a good got damn for any...

BENNET: That's what I said. What do I give a good got
damn for! I said this is my own little space and the
world ain't coming in here. But it comes anyway. I got
this piece of paper that means nothing! I might as well
wipe my ass with it cause it ain't opening no doors,

nobody's saying "Well sit right here Mister Moore, sit here with that beautiful sheepskin and thrill us! Lay down that piece of paper that says you know what we know and join the community of men! Nobody's saying nothing, but in that room I got black olives make you cry and Sunday mornings and the world still comes in, it lays in your bed and when it's finished doing its business the crossword ain't worth shit!

SYLVESTER: You looking for pity cause you in here cutting heads?

BENNET: I'm telling you what sent me running up in here. I'm trying to tell you something.

SYLVESTER: *(Laughing hard)* Look here, Harold, the professor trying to tell me something! He come home full of facts and a fresh ass whipping, but he wanna tell me something. I'm on my third life, boy! Cause I was a porter? 'Cause I ain't make it nothing more, nothing less than a living? I fed my family, kept a roof over they heads from leaking like a scive and falling in. When that door opens all the man wanna know is, can you cut a head. That's all he wanna know. But you wanna tell me something.

BENNET: *(He throws over the card table, dominoes fly everywhere.)* Get on the train or get left!

SYLVESTER: Negro have you lost yo'...!

NATE: *(Paper down, looking out the window)* Here come Claude!

(CLAUDE flies in the door, shuts it behind him and leans on it, exhausted, breathing hard.)

HAROLD: *(Throws up his hands in resignation)* Shit.

SYLVESTER: Where's Wilmot?

CLAUDE: *(To BENNET)* You should'a come with me!

HAROLD: I'm moving, I'm moving to Balti...

SYLVESTER: Where is Tuck Wilmot!

CLAUDE: *(Still breathing hard, excited)* You should'a seen the look on his face. That's what I wanted. That look like you would crawl back in your mama if she was standing there cause what you're looking at is real. Real! I could have left right then but some people walked in and...

HAROLD: Some people! What you mean some people?

CLAUDE: ...and it was too late.

SYLVESTER: Too late...

CLAUDE: Soon as he seen them come in, his face, changed, went back to what we been looking at since we been drawing breath, like that day with Louis, that "strolling to the car face." And Quincey put him down.

SYLVESTER: Quincey?

CLAUDE: He was there when I showed up! You should'a seen him!

HAROLD: *(Comes away from the window)* You know how big Baltimore is. Trolley cars and...

(The door opens and FRANK *steps in. Every one is still. He closes the door.)*

FRANK: We got us a mess, Sylvester.

SYLVESTER: Little bit.

FRANK: Little bit?! I thought I told you to keep a lid on this and the whole damn pot done come off the stove! I got a dead white man, Sylvester. A dead White man! You lucky every house this side of town ain't burning.

SYLVESTER: Quincey had a right.

FRANK: Quincey is laying over to the hardware store right now waiting on George Clifford! I walk out of here with Claude and we might be able to...

SYLVESTER: We cain't do that.

FRANK: *(Laughs. Slowly moving closer to* CLAUDE, *who isn't moving at all)* Sylvester what are you all drinking in here! Now you turn around and let me put these cuffs on you Claude 'cause I guaranty you, you don't walk out of here with me won't none of you be leaving here!

(The door flies open and CHI-TOWN *stumbles in, hair wild, clothes disheveled, knife in hand. He doesn't bother to shut the door.)*

*(*CHI-TOWN *moves quickly for* CLAUDE *and* CLAUDE *moves towards him. Everyone moves aside except* FRANK *who attempts to stay between the two men, hands up.)*

CHI-TOWN: Huh? Nobody at the table? I come for my game home-boy, I come for my game!

(He flies at CLAUDE, FRANK *still in the middle. There is a scuffle for a moment then none of the three men moves.* CLAUDE *and* CHI-TOWN *back away and leave* FRANK, *stabbed.* FRANK *looks bewildered, then drops to his knees, holding the handle of the knife.)*

HAROLD: *(Throws up his hands)* Aww naw!

FRANK: *(Laughing)* You done gone from bad to worse. Just somebody call Meeks.

(Nobody moves. He screams.)

FRANK: I said call Meeks!

*(*HAROLD *moves for the phone and* SYLVESTER *stops him.)*

SYLVESTER: Meeks ain't coming here. Not for this.

FRANK: *(Pulls out his gun but cannot raise it)* You don't call Meeks I'm gonna shoot everybody in here. You tell'em, Syl, this looks bad. Tuck Wilmot is one thing, *but the law.* I tell you, you kill the law and the world falls apart. You hear me, it falls apart! You get on that phone and you call Meeks you hear me you call Meeks!

SYLVESTER: Get out. Everybody get out. Go to Boston or Baltimore or Chicago, go to France. Just get the hell out of here.

BENNET: Mister Sylvester, you...

SYLVESTER: You thought that ass whipping you come home with was bad! You better get on. People be here any minute.

BENNET: I'm not leaving.

CHI-TOWN: Damn! Don't nothing go like it supposed to down here!

SYLVESTER: *(Pulls a chair up next to the fading* FRANK*)* We go back, don't we, Frank.

FRANK: You damn right! I cut you out that tree, whatn't for me you wouldn't have nothing to go back to!

SYLVESTER: Saved my life once. I figure, I return the favor.

FRANK: *(Leans side to side, then forward)* Sylvester, call Meeks. You ain't making no sense.

SYLVESTER: Can't...

FRANK: Yes! Yes you can you 'member, we was young and I I saved you from that tree me Sylvester whatn't for me...

SYLVESTER: You bought me! Like you buy a pair of shoes. Bought me. All these years I been feeling funny and I swear it just hit me, I ain't seen Sylvester since that day, 'bout to go up that tree!

FRANK: You crazy! Everybody in Durham know I'm here. Somebody's gonna come....

SYLVESTER: I feel kind'a good. I missed myself.

(Phone rings.)

BENNET: Willy's Cut and Shine...I'm sorry Helen....

HAROLD: *(He reaches for the phone.)* I'm here. Helen...
Right, right...I'll be right there. Syl, I, I...Helen waiting
on me, she say a bunch of folk just went by the house
and...

SYLVESTER: Go on, Harold. Thirty two years you ain't
won a game. And you sho' ain't about to win this one.

*(HAROLD hesitates, then exits. CLAUDE follows him to the
door.)*

CLAUDE: *(At the window)* The hawk is sho'nuff flying
today.

CHI-TOWN: I guess we just gone wait.

BENNET: Not like before. Won't never be like it was
before.

*(Pause. FRANK falls forward then to his side, dead.
SYLVESTER picks up the gun and moves to the window
and looks out. Lights dim and QUINCEY, in his bare feet,
enter from one side down stage and LOLAR from the other.)*

QUINCEY: You see me? I'm clean.

LOLAR: What I tell ya'? Don't matter how you cut'em
they ruin yo' feet. We home now, Q.

QUINCEY: We home.

LOLAR: *(Looks off-stage, anxious to exit.)* You hear'em Q?
Harlem! They waiting on us!

QUINCEY: I gotta stay, Louis still here, and the ground is
'bout to open up.

LOLAR: Listen to'em! Spring time in Harlem! Sink our
teeth right down to the seed!...me, you, Cooper...you
got all eternity, fall into oblivion...come on...

QUINCEY: I'm gonna plant Louis and he's gonna come
up good. Like I told you--he gone come up like one
them redwoods!

LOLAR: *(Breaks out in jubilance)* "You better come on, in my kitchen..." I see you in Harlem, Q'!

QUINCEY: See you in Harlem.

(Black out)

END OF PLAY

www.ingramcontent.com/pod-product-compliance
Lightning Source LLC
Chambersburg PA
CBHW052212090426
42741CB00010B/2512